Coffee

Coffee

A cultural history from around the world

Ed S. Milton

Astrolog Publishing House Ltd.

Edited by: S. Milton
Cover Design: Na'ama Yaffe
Layout and Graphics: Daniel Akerman

P.O. Box 1123, Hod Hasharon 45111, Israel
Tel: 972-9-7412044
Fax: 972-9-7442714

ISBN 965-494-158-9

Published by Astrolog Publishing House 2003

10 9 8 7 6 5 4 3 2 1

*T*he first evidence of "coffee" comes to us from the Moslem world, from countries such as the Yemen on the Red Sea coast. In the Yemen grew a plant that had originated in the Kaffa province in Ethiopia. Ethiopian Christians who emigrated to the Yemen brought the plant with them, built a monastery, and planted the coffee trees around it. Some time later, the Moslem herdsmen in the Yemen began to complain that the goats and donkeys that ate the plant "went crazy." In 1670, a regulation was passed in the Yemen, stating that coffee trees had to be fenced in with a fence as high as "the height of a man and a half."

*I*n books and encyclopedias that were published at the end of the 17th century and the beginning of the 18th century, coffee trees were linked to goats for the simple reason that goat droppings resemble coffee beans, and at that time, the opinion that similar = the same = similar prevailed.

*C*offee is sacred to Moslems as a result of the legend that the Angel Gabriel offered the Prophet Muhammed, who was suffering from exhaustion, an unknown beverage that immediately revived him. This beverage, which was as black as the stone of the Ka'ba in Mecca, and tasted bitter, was called k'hawah.

lack coffee replaced wine in the Moslem world, since wine-drinking had been forbidden by Muhammed. Coffee is sometimes known as "the wine of the Moslems."

*T*he first known use of coffee beans was not for drinking but as a paste that was masticated in some regions of Africa and in Arab countries. It was, in fact, the first energy pill. In 1253, a Jewish physician who worked in what is known as Syria today wrote a prescription for the ruler, who would fall asleep prior to  performing his conjugal duties: "After the prayers… chew five beans of *k'hawah* until they turn into a paste, and smear this paste over your belly before getting into bed…"

Many physicians in the first millennium CE believed that there was a plant called kaffa, and drinking an essence produced from its beans… prevented crying! "It is not possible to cry after drinking a cup of black coffee," wrote a Moslem physician in the 13th century. In the same context, incidentally, the doctors mentioned that wine is a beverage that stimulates crying and tears.

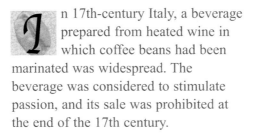 n 17th-century Italy, a beverage prepared from heated wine in which coffee beans had been marinated was widespread. The beverage was considered to stimulate passion, and its sale was prohibited at the end of the 17th century.

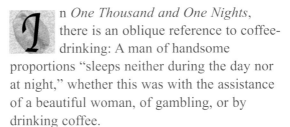

*I*n *One Thousand and One Nights*, there is an oblique reference to coffee-drinking: A man of handsome proportions "sleeps neither during the day nor at night," whether this was with the assistance of a beautiful woman, of gambling, or by drinking coffee.

*A*lthough coffee was known centuries before he was born, the German chemist Runge is considered to be the person who discovered caffeine, the active ingredient in coffee.

*T*oday, coffee is directly linked to caffeine, but there are many places in the world where the sources of caffeine are not actually in coffee beans. In Africa, the cola-nut or the cyclopia (wild tea) plant are used. In South America, there are many plant seeds and maté leaves that are rich in caffeine.

*C*old coffee is not a 20th-century invention. The first coffee beverage in Africa was prepared from a liquid that was obtained from fresh coffee beans and cold water. The Arabs were the  ones who got the world accustomed to drinking coffee made with boiling water.

Moslem tradition attributes the discovery of the coffee beverage to a prince called Omarin. He was fleeing from his enemies in the desert and, hungry and thirsty, reached an oasis, where he fell asleep under a tall tree. In the morning, he gathered some of the fruits from the tree in a vessel and tried to eat them, but they were too hard. He poured a little water over them and tried to soften them, but the fruits remained hard, and the prince made do with drinking only the water… To his surprise, he was filled with energy and renewed strength.

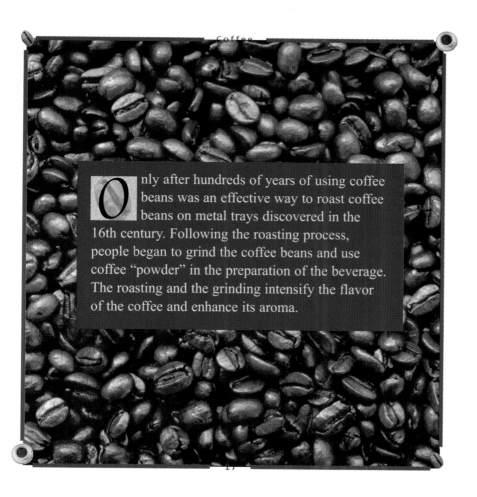

Only after hundreds of years of using coffee beans was an effective way to roast coffee beans on metal trays discovered in the 16th century. Following the roasting process, people began to grind the coffee beans and use coffee "powder" in the preparation of the beverage. The roasting and the grinding intensify the flavor of the coffee and enhance its aroma.

*T*he Arabs prepare coffee in a jug that is called a *jibrik*, which is actually a special kettle for boiling coffee. In this jug, coffee is boiled along with sugar and spices such as cinnamon.

*C*offee houses, as they are known in the West, began in Turkey. They were actually pleasure houses, lavishly furnished and in quiet places, whose goal was to pamper their clients – men – and help them forget their day-to-day worries.

*I*n parallel to the public coffee houses, a coffee-drinking ceremony began to develop in the Middle East – a ceremony that was similar to the tea-drinking ceremony in Japan, but less strict in its rules. In this ceremony, which was meant for men, a man prepared the coffee in a long ceremony, during the course of which many greetings were exchanged, prayers uttered, and long conversations held.

*I*n 17th-century Turkey, a woman could divorce her husband if he neglected his duty of … supplying coffee to her kitchen. In 1737, a wealthy merchant was found guilty of not supplying the women in his harem with coffee, and he was forced to divorce all of them.

*A*t the end of the 17th century, the Turks fought against the city of Vienna and besieged its walls. With a great military effort and with the help of its allies, Austria defeated the Turks and routed its army –

some half-million warriors. The loot found by the Austrians in the Turkish camps included 1,700 sacks of green-brown seeds that were unfamiliar to them. A Polish mercenary who knew the Turks and had fought for Vienna received the sacks as his portion of the loot. Within a year, he introduced coffee-drinking into Vienna and became the wealthiest merchant in the city.

*T*here are coffee houses there where they prepare coffee in large jugs for dozens of guests. The coffee houses are the common domain of guests (men) from the various social classes. On the balconies of the coffee houses, mattresses are spread around for reclining, and generally, during peak hours, there are musicians and singers who appear there. It is a custom that

anyone who reclines in the coffee house invites the ones who enter to drink their first cup of coffee at his expense. The owner of the coffee house is called Jaba, which means 'gratis'

[From the book of travels to the Middle East by J. D. Thèrenot, 1644]

*A*t the end of the 17th century, peddlers known by the name of candiot appeared in the cities of Turkey and the East. On their backs, they carried giant jugs of coffee, heated with charcoal, which they poured into cups that they sold to people in the streets or in houses. When this fashion reached the West, the peddlers were called "human coffee houses."

Drink of love

Divine providence revealed its secret.
Wine gladdens the human heart,
But good coffee is ten times as good.

*J*ohann Sebastian Bach composed the humorous Coffee Cantata, which centered around coffee. It tells the story of a dispute between the ruler, who wants to prohibit coffee-drinking because the beverage causes sorrow and grief, and women who are prepared to give up bread… but not coffee. Bach got the idea for the composition from a tale by Picander.

*N*apoleon, a coffee addict, wrote in his diary: "They always prepare several jugs of coffee on the fire for me, since I need coffee in order to remain awake at night and go over the paperwork."

olitical circumstances were what caused the coffee/chicory seed war. Chicory is a plant that grows in Europe, and when Europe lost contact with the colonies and with their coffee plantations, experiments were conducted to find substitutes for coffee. In France and Germany, an attempt was made to dry and grind chicory seeds and produce a coffee substitute. The news of the chicory substitute was publicized by the wife of a chicory merchant in Europe. She claimed that the chicory beverage – the

coffee substitute – had cured her of nervousness and conditions of hysteria. When Napoleon adopted the chicory beverage as a substitute for coffee, the golden age of coffee substitutes began. During World War I, chicory served as a substitute for coffee as a beverage throughout Europe.

*O*ver the course of hundreds of years, hundreds of seeds, roots and fruits were tested as possible coffee substitutes. Today, hundreds of coffee substitutes, from dahlia tubers to box seeds, are available.

*I*n the Prussian army in the mid-19th century, there were soldiers whose entire job was to tote jugs of coffee on their backs and pour cupfuls for the other soldiers. According to the orders, there had to be one "coffee bearer" for every 40 combat soldiers.

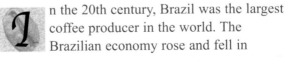

In the 20th century, Brazil was the largest coffee producer in the world. The Brazilian economy rose and fell in accordance with coffee prices and crops. In good years, Brazil exported some 25 million sacks of coffee, and even more importantly, the inhabitants of Brazil themselves drank about 10 million sacks of coffee – more than the total amount exported by the second largest coffee exporter, Colombia.

*C*olombia exports about a quarter of the amount of sacks that Brazil exports, but its advantage lies in the quality and not in the quantity. The coffee trees in Colombia grow in the high regions, and the coffee beans are considered superb.

n Africa, the
largest coffee
exporter is
Angola (the fourth
largest exporter in the
world). In Angola,
coffee is grown in large
plantations managed by
international companies.

*I*ndia produces about two million sacks of coffee per annum, about half of it for local consumption. Coffee-growing in India is secondary to that of tea.

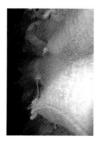

ndonesia produces about a million sacks of coffee per annum, but the quality of the coffee, which is known as Java, is such that there is a great demand for Indonesian coffee, and its price is high accordingly.

*T*he more finely the coffee beans are ground, the greater the area of contact of the beans with the water, and the shorter the preparation time. Coffee experts have determined four degrees of bean size, from the finest, which requires three minutes of contact with water, to the coarsest, which requires nine minutes. The required time, in intervals of two minutes, determines the "grinding." Grinders in trading houses in Europe are marked 3, 5, 7 or 9 according to the size of the grains they produce.

A summary of alternative medicine (with a touch of "Grandma's remedies") says that coffee stimulates and strengthens respiration, increases the heartbeat rate, raises blood pressure, and speeds up digestion as well as the excretion of feces and urine. All that is positive.

*C*offee, according to alternative medicine, is not recommended for hot-tempered and nervous people, for people who suffer from hypertension, for people who suffer from heart diseases, or for people who suffer from heartburn and bleeding ulcers in the digestive tract.

*B*y the way, alternative medicine (and conventional medicine as well) recognizes the phenomenon of "coffee poisoning" that is caused by drinking too much coffee.

*G*round coffee spoils when exposed to light or comes into contact with the air, so it should be stored in a dark sealed container, preferably in the refrigerator. For lengthy storage, it can be kept in the freezer.

round coffee, even in excellent
storage conditions, loses its flavor
after about a year.

offee beans keep better and longer than ground coffee.

*G*rinding coffee beans prior to preparing the coffee stresses the aroma and maximizes the flavor.

*H*eating the coffee beans prior to grinding them strengthens the aroma of the ground coffee.

n order to strengthen the aroma of the coffee, you can add – before pouring the water over it – a tiny pinch of … salt.

piece of advice to anyone who is preparing coffee and wants to "cheat" with the taste: When the taste of the coffee and its aroma are too strong, add a little bit of … hot cocoa to it. And when the taste and the aroma of the coffee are weak and indiscernible, add… a teaspoonful of instant coffee to it!

manual coffee-grinder preserves the taste of the coffee much better than an electric grinder.

*T*he quality of the water that is used for preparing the coffee is no less important than the quality of the coffee itself. "Fresh" water (that is, water that has not been standing in a container for a long time) must be used, and must be poured onto the coffee as soon as the water boils (it must not boil for a long time).

*N*ot all coffee merchants will be happy to read this tip. When you buy coffee, fill a large glass with water and pour a teaspoon of the coffee into it. The coffee grounds will float on the water. If there are other substances in the coffee, such as chicory, roasted beans and so on, they will sink in the water. If you want quality, make sure that the coffee grounds float on top of the water.

*A*nd what do we do with the coffee residues in the cup or the pot, besides reading coffee grounds? This is one of the best fertilizers for house plants.

t's good to know that in a glass of cola there is about half of the amount of caffeine that there is in a large cup of good filter coffee (about 100 mg).

n an identical quantity of tea and coffee, there is a quarter to a half more caffeine in coffee than in tea.

*W*omen know that the way to a man's heart is often through a friendly cup of coffee. They don't all know that coffee (more precisely, caffeine), is also a "pregnancy inhibitor." There is no basis whatsoever to the claim that five cups of coffee a day serve as an effective contraceptive (unless you grow the coffee tree yourself, nurture it, gather the coffee beans, roast them and grind them… and then you don't have time to get pregnant!). However, most experts agree that drinking five cups of coffee a day can prevent the fertilized ovum from developing further.

A cup of coffee is an excellent preventive measure against… tooth decay! Coffee contains a substance that prevents plaque from accumulating on the enamel of the tooth. The result may be stained teeth – but with no cavities!

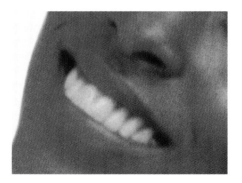

Some alternative medicine experts claim that caffeine (especially in coffee, where there is a high concentration) can be beneficial to asthmatics, since it expands the respiratory tracts. Most of them recommend black coffee without milk.

*A*s many people are aware, a cup of strong coffee (or a cup of "black" tea) relieves headaches. The scientific explanation is that caffeine shrinks and regulates the expansion of the blood vessels (in the head) that create the feeling of pain because of excessive expansion.

A cup of coffee increases the powers of concentration and thinking, but this only works for a short time. The good effect lasts for about an hour, reaches its peak after an hour and quickly subsides during the subsequent half-hour.

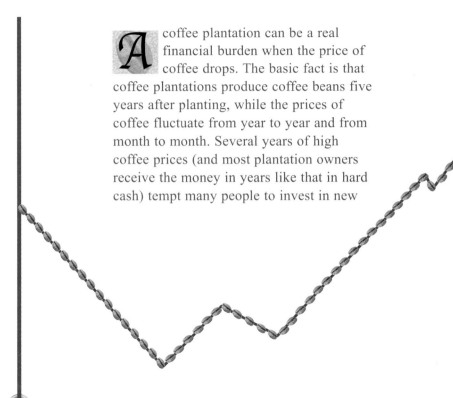

A coffee plantation can be a real financial burden when the price of coffee drops. The basic fact is that coffee plantations produce coffee beans five years after planting, while the prices of coffee fluctuate from year to year and from month to month. Several years of high coffee prices (and most plantation owners receive the money in years like that in hard cash) tempt many people to invest in new coffee plantations. A few years later, there is a huge supply and if there isn't a commensurate rise in demand, the prices plummet sharply. The plantation owners lose their capital, uproot the coffee trees and look for another more profitable crop... It is well known that many countries have suffered from crises in coffee prices that were so serious that they caused the governments and the countries to collapse.

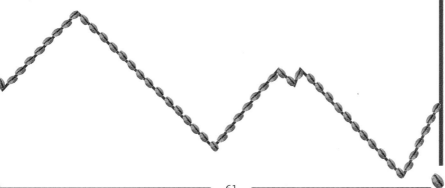

On the same topic: A children's story from Brazil tells of two brothers. One of them raised corn and the other raised coffee trees, and they both brought sacks filled with their crops home. The corn grower was happy and sang all the way – now he had corn to eat, corn to feed his livestock, corn to make a drink from and corn to sell… The coffee grower, however, wept fearfully all the way home –

all he owned was coffee beans, and he didn't know what price he'd get for them! He couldn't eat them, he couldn't feed them to his livestock, and if he drank them, he wouldn't be able to sleep at night and his worries would grow. This story illustrates more than anything the dependence of the coffee-growing industry on the taste and demand for the coffee beverage.

*C*offee beans were among the first products that were traded on the modern stock exchange. This process began with a public auction of sacks of coffee beans by Arab merchants (who controlled the coffee market until the 18th century) and by the Dutch. Amsterdam was the center for the sale of coffee beans imported from the Far East by the Dutch East India Company. When the center for the trade in coffee beans shifted London, the modern exchange for trading goods began to emerge.

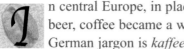 n central Europe, in places where men drank mainly beer, coffee became a woman's drink. Gossip in the German jargon is *kaffeeklatsch* – "what you talk about over a cup of coffee," and the expression *kaffeeschwester* actually means "a gossip." Perhaps this is the reason why many limitations were imposed on the opening of cafés in Germany in the 18th and 19th centuries.

n the 17th and 18th centuries, coffee was called "Black Apollo" in France and was linked in various ways to sexuality. A French wall newspaper called for the outlawing of coffee because "a woman who drinks black coffee is liable to succumb to temptation and commit adultery even with black-skinned slaves…"

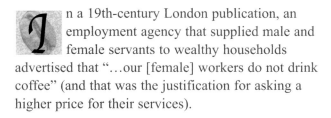 n a 19th-century London publication, an employment agency that supplied male and female servants to wealthy households advertised that "…our [female] workers do not drink coffee" (and that was the justification for asking a higher price for their services).

*I*n a London bankruptcy court in the 18th century, the owner of a carriage service company claimed that he could not pay his debts because his "three daughters had become addicted to the black brew, and used up a whole tin of the coffee from the pantry every single day." Every day he spent "an amount of money on coffee that would suffice to maintain a stable full of horses…"

On bended knee, the black slaves of the Ambassador, arrayed in the most gorgeous Oriental costumes served the choicest Mocha coffee in tiny cups of egg-shell porcelain, hot, strong and fragrant, poured out in saucers of gold and silver, placed on embroidered silk doylies fringed with gold bullion, to the grand dames, who fluttered their fans with many grimaces, bending their piquant faces – be-rouged, be-powdered and be-patched – over the new and steaming beverages.

Isaac D'Israeli, "Curiosities of Literature"

*B*uy the coffee berries at any druggist for approximately three shillings for a pound. Put any quantity of berries in an old frying pan. Put the pan over a charcoal fire and keep stirring until the berries are black. Crack one open with your teeth to check that they're as black inside as they are out. However, if they are overcooked, the oil that makes the drink is wasted, but keep cooking the berries until they are white – you won't get coffee, but you will be able to use the salt from the berries. Once the berries are properly cooked (till black both inside and out), mash them through a sieve, and they are ready to be used.

A recipe for roasting coffee from the 17th century:

*J*ohn Ernest McCann: "Coffee makes a sad man cheerful; a languourous man, active; a cold man, warm; a warm man, glowing; a debilitated man, strong. It intoxicates, without inviting the police; it excites a flow of spirits, and awakens mental powers thought to be dead.... When coffee is bad, it is the wickedest thing in town;

when good, the most glorious. When it has lost its aromatic flavor and appeals no more to the eye, smell, or taste, it is fierie; but when left in a sick room, with the lid off, it fills the room with a fragrance only jacqueminots can rival. The very smell of coffee in a sick room terrorizes death."

"Over the Black Coffee" an almanac by Arthur Gray (1902)

May the drink that I love,
Rule by divine right!
Wean the wine drinker from his grape;
You are far better than wine!

A song sung in Greek by a coffee vendor who went from
house to house selling cups of black coffee (1690)

Coffee, which makes the politican wise,
And see thro' all things with his half-shut eyes.

Alexander Pope, Rape of the Lock

For those with little wit
Coffee is a brightener.
The most barren of authors
Is made fertile by it.
It has in it a virtue
Strengthening the memory,
So that a pedant can talk,

Without rhyme or reason,
Spouting fable and history.
Coffee works a miracle,
Sharpening the brains of the stupid.
No author refreshed by it
Need languish in silence.
Coffee's strength and virtue
Double the memory.
Every drop empowers us
To gabble continuously,
And, discarding the crutches of rhyme,
To spout fable as history.

About how coffee can make anyone intelligent and
can turn anyone into a poet (18th century)

"*G*reat is the vogue of coffee in Paris. In the houses where it is supplied, the proprietors know how to prepare it in such a way that it gives wit to those who drink it. At any rate, when they depart, all of them believe themselves to be at least four times as brainy as when they entered the doors."

Montesquieu, Lettres persanes (18th century)

This gentle vapor that rises in clouds
Will develop for us, la, la,
Our imagination, tum, tum,
To produce a fine work.

The coffee fumes from public places neutralized conflicting opinions (18th century)

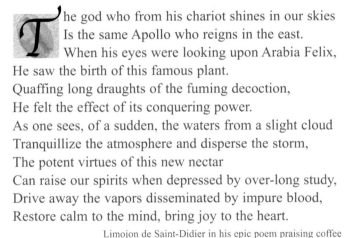

*T*he god who from his chariot shines in our skies
Is the same Apollo who reigns in the east.
When his eyes were looking upon Arabia Felix,
He saw the birth of this famous plant.
Quaffing long draughts of the fuming decoction,
He felt the effect of its conquering power.
As one sees, of a sudden, the waters from a slight cloud
Tranquillize the atmosphere and disperse the storm,
The potent virtues of this new nectar
Can raise our spirits when depressed by over-long study,
Drive away the vapors disseminated by impure blood,
Restore calm to the mind, bring joy to the heart.

Limojon de Saint-Didier in his epic poem praising coffee

ellow-countryman and hero, in the springtime of thy life,
Undaunted didst thou steer thy ship through the storm,
Conveying to the new world the glorious plant
That gives our blood fresh life
And enriches our fatherland.

Excerpt of a poem to the memory of Captain Desclieux by the periodical L'Annee litteraire.

"Coffee, the sobering beverage, a mighty nutriment of the brain, unlike spirituous liquors, increases purity and clarity; coffee, which at length substitutes stimulation of the mind for stimulation of the sexual faculties!…The strong coffee of San Domingo, which Buffon, Diderot, and Rousseau drank, redoubled the ardor of their ardent souls – and the prophets who assembled day after day in the Cafe Procope saw, with penetrating glance, in the depths of their black drink the illumination of the year of the revolution."

Michelet (historian) who wrote about the intellectual life of the 18th century.

It is of unrivalled value
In maladies of the heart;
The pineal gland
Is fortified by it.

Sung in the streets of Paris long before the French revolution.

No lover shall woo me
Unless I have his pledge,
Written in the marriage settlement,
That he will allow me
To drink coffee when I please.

Johann Sebastian Bach, Coffee Cantata

The news comes from Paris: A few short days ago
An edict was issued, The king, you Germans must know,]
Declared his will thuswise: "We have, to our grief and pain,
Learned that coffee wreaks ruin and does terrific bane.
To heal the grievous disaster, We hereby declare

That none to drink this same coffee in future shall dare,
Save Us and Our court, and the greatly privileged few
To whom, in Our royal kindness, We leave may endue.
Without such a permit, the drink is unlawful."
Hereupon there resounded a clamor most awful.
"Alas!" cried the women, "take rather our bread.
Can't live without coffee. We'll all soon be dead!"
But the king would not budge, nor his edict revise;
And, lo, as predicted, his subjects died off like flies;
Interments were wholesale, as if from the pest;
Girls, grannies, and mothers with babes at their breast,
Until the king, becoming more and more afraid,
At length cancelled his edict, and then the plague was stayed.

Picander, Parisian Fables, 1727 – a skit on the debate about coffee.

"I always had seven coffee-pots on the boil while I was discussing with the Turks, for I had to stay awake all night talking over religious matters with them."

Napoleon, talking about his experiences during the Egyptian campaign.

O Coffee, thou dispersest sorrow,
Thou art the drink of the faithful,
Thou givest health to those who labor,
And enablest the good to find the truth.
O Coffee, thou art our gold!
There, where thou art offered,
Men grow good and wise.
May Allah overthrow thy calumniators
And deliver thee from their wiles.

Shekh Abd el Kader in Envoy

Predicting The Future Using Coffee Grounds

Foretelling the future through coffee grounds - or reading the past and the present - is an ancient art form. It bears a strong resemblance to other forms of mysticism and prophecy such as palm reading, stargazing, dream interpretation, and card reading. But, there is also an essential difference.

Coffee reading is very difficult to learn. In contrast to other methods of prophecy, most of whose "secrets" can be learned through courses or books, the reading of coffee grounds demands a much higher degree of sensitivity and intuition - an inner force that takes over and guides the coffee reader. It is very hard to teach the secret of this sensitivity or this ability to act as a medium. This is perhaps why there are almost no basic, in-depth works devoted to the reading of coffee grounds.

Why can one person read coffee while another sees nothing more in the grounds than dirt to be washed down the drain? To understand this, we must go back to childhood. Children like to look up at the clouds and imagine different shapes.

One child will see an entire world in the clouds, while another sees nothing but the clouds themselves! That, in a nutshell, is the difference. The coffee reader does not really see anything in the usual visual sense; she sees everything solely through her inner eye. Not everybody has the capability to be a medium.

To see things in the grounds, the reader must attain a combination of euphoria and deep relaxation - a feeling of remoteness, of floating, of slipping out of the boundaries of the body and soul. Once the reader has achieved this state, the eye itself must learn to see things, yet be detached from what it sees. As children, we would look at the clouds and say, "Here's a bear, here's an elephant, here's the Eiffel Tower." All of the pictures were interwoven, dissolving into one another, and we would "see" an entire world. Look at the coffee grounds as if they are a blue sky studded with clouds. Note the sign, the first shape that comes to mind - without trying to think about or understand it.

Acrobat - An acrobat, in the form of a tumbler or gymnast, always symbolizes a love affair, especially if the querent is a woman. In the case of a man, the interpretation would be a love affair involving a woman connected to him. Many acrobats in one formation of coffee grounds change the picture into an actual circus...or a real orgy!

Banana - The banana, due to its suggestive shape, is always associated with sex. In most cases, it is interpreted as infidelity or a significant sexual problem (especially if the querent is a male). The precise explanation must take into account the total picture. A peeled banana indicates that the problem is getting worse.

Bat - A significant formation. It indicates that the querent is well-schooled in disappointment, and is constantly fearful that people - even close friends - are constantly plotting against him. It is difficult to offer a possible solution. In a woman's cup, a bat also symbolizes the fear of a varied sex life, and the desperate clinging to the normal and the ordinary in her life.

Bee - Financial success on a large scale awaits the seeker. His riches will gain him fame and glory on the social front. Always a good sign. For a woman, it can suggest marriage to a wealthy man. The interpretation remains the same whether we see a single bee or a swarm.

Bow - A bow, with or without an arrow, suggests a love affair which revealed the uglier sides of the querent's character - nasty gossip, wrongful treatment of the partner, etc. If this formation is seen in a woman's cup, in relation to a question about her partner, she should keep her eyes open and be careful! A simple formation that can tell a lot about the querent and his/her environment. It appears primarily in the grounds of women.

Butterfly - Capriciousness, a certain degree of hypocrisy - but not in extreme form. Numerous sexual experiences. Important: this formation indicates that the querent stretches - but does not cross - the boundaries of good taste.

Cherry - One or more cherries (usually a pair) always relate to a love affair. In a woman's cup, a cherry indicates a past love affair which she recalls to this day. For a man, it signifies the almost obsessive pursuit of women. The cherry, incidentally, is associated with virginity: in a man's cup, it suggests a desire to win the hand of a virgin; in the case of a woman, it points to sexual trauma.

Chest - Generally appears in the form of a woman's breasts, but can also be a man's chest. This formation signifies the pursuit of true love (not necessarily sexual in nature). In women, it can also indicate the desire to have a child.

Circle - A circle, which sometimes appears in the form of a ring, relates to love or marriage, and appears primarily in the coffee grounds of women. An intact circle symbolizes romantic success, marriage, reconciliation with a romantic partner, and the like. A broken circle signifies problems in these same areas. A circle with a small hill in the center (resembling a breast viewed from above) means that the birth of a child will affect the querent. This does not necessarily refer to the birth of the querent's own child!

Dove - A very lucky sign! A dove is always a good formation...and unfortunately quite a rare one. A dove in the cup of a young woman about to marry is a truly outstanding sign!

Egg - A good sign. When several eggs appear together, the sign is reinforced. An egg symbolizes prosperity, success in love, a (wanted) pregnancy in the near future. Note the shapes close to the egg in order to know in which sphere the success will occur. When an unusually large egg appears in the grounds of a man or a woman, this indicates prolonged sexual frustration. A cracked or broken egg weakens the sign to a great extent.

Fork - Someone close to you is betraying you. Beware of insincere speeches. (Some readers take this a step further: a fork with two tines indicates an unfaithful man, while three tines signify an unfaithful woman.)

Fountain - An excellent sign! Success, wealth and happiness in all areas of life. Boundless sexuality. Romance. A formation that is always positive.

Giraffe - Impulsiveness in thought and deed leads to unexpected complications. The querent must weigh every decision carefully. Pay special attention to the position of the giraffe's head - its direction can suggest the area in which the trouble will occur. Incidentally, a giraffe adjacent to a figure with sexual significance has a different interpretation: problems in bed - and major ones!

Groom - A groom always signifies...divorce! We don't know in what way the querent will be connected with the divorce - he/she might be going through a divorce, he/she might be the cause of someone else's divorce, etc. - but it is clear that a divorce will affect his/her life.

Heart - A good sign, especially in matters pertaining to love or, even more so, marriage. A heart is always whole, and always has a positive interpretation. A broken heart is not revealed through the heart shape itself, but through adjacent formations. The size of the heart has no significance. A heart shape suspended from a special chain indicates subjugation to another person as a result of love.

Horse - The horse is a formation frequently encountered by coffee readers. In principle, it is a positive figure, especially when seen to be galloping. The hindquarters of a horse are likely to indicate that success lies beyond reach. A figure on horseback means that the querent has a loyal partner or companion. A horse's head indicates a daring love affair...or life in the shadow of danger!

Kettle - A kettle suggests minor illnesses, but also has sexual connotations (especially if the spout is visible). In the grounds of both a man and a woman, a kettle indicates sexual problems on the part of a male, with regard to his performance as well as the shape and size of his genitals.

Lemon - In a man's cup, a lemon formation indicates love of women; in a woman's cup, the lemon indicates disappointment in men.

Matches - Many unsatisfying love affairs. A formation that is not flattering to the querent.

Necklace - If the necklace is whole, the querent's relationship with his or her partner is stable and positive; if it is torn apart, a problem is creating distance between the partners. The size of the gap between the ends indicates the extent of the problem. This is a problem that can always be solved.

Octopus - An octopus, taken by itself, is a bad sign. It tells the person that he must seek the help of others in solving his problems. Interestingly enough, the sexual interpretation is unhappiness at the absence of a meaningful relationship, for a woman; or serious problems involving sexual expression, for a man. Incidentally, in the grounds of children, or that refer to children, an octopus indicates repressed fears or severe traumas. It is important to look into this!

Olive - A significant formation. Generally appears in the form of a branch, which is identifiable by the shape of the leaves and fruit. In a man's cup, it points to serious sexual problems; in a woman's cup, it suggests troubling sexual memories from her past. In both cases, the reader must interpret the future (regardless of where in the cup the formation appears) as better than the past. In the cup of a sick person, the olive is a sign of healing and long life.

Package - A common formation. A package generally indicates a surprise for the querent in the near future. We do not know exactly what kind of surprise - it is very difficult to give either a positive or a negative interpretation. A different explanation, in the case of a man asking about a woman, relates to the package's presentation: a package that is tied up signifies an upright woman, even a virgin, whereas an open package suggests a woman with hidden sexual urges.

Person - A formation in the shape of a person is one of the hardest signs to interpret. The figure itself can take several different forms: a man or a woman, an old person or a child. We tend to interpret male or female figures in the contexts of love, sex, marriage or divorce - male-female relationships - and the interpretations of figures of children or old people focus mainly on health.

When the querent is a man, figures of a woman or women indicate sexual or romantic ties. The coffee reader must interpret the figures and their status carefully, based on other formations. If only male figures are present in a male querent's cup, we can deduce that he has homosexual tendencies - or that he is a cuckold. The presence of many female figures indicates that he is a Casanova. Since several figures, of both sexes, often appear in coffee grounds, you must steer your way carefully among the various interpretations.

When the querent is a woman, the basic principle is the same. If only female figures appear in the grounds, either she has lesbian tendencies or women have had an inordinate influence in her life. Numerous male figures mean that she is a flirt. A lone male figure signifies the one great love of her life!

The presence of many figures complicates the picture. If, for example, in a man's cup, we see the figures of a man and a

woman, this may mean that his lover is having an affair on the side...or that his parents had a decisive influence on his life. So, much caution is needed here!

The interpretation of human figures is a rather advanced stage of coffee reading, and requires much experience. As a rule, the reader should first interpret all the symbols that appear in the grounds, and only then look at the human figures. Be extremely cautious!

Pineapple - A pineapple mainly says something about the querent's personality; it signifies a person who is involved in many arguments and minor disputes, but also tends to seek reconciliation and compromise with his opponents after every quarrel. When the querent is a woman, a pineapple indicates the presence of many suitors or lovers in her life.

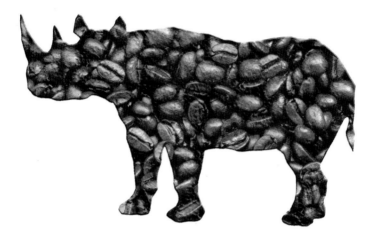

Rhinoceros - This formation appears only in women's grounds, and its meaning is sexual incompatibility between the woman and her partner...due to a problem on the man's part (always!).

Ring - In general, a ring signifies marriage. If the ring is whole, a marriage will take place shortly, or the future of an existing marriage is assured. A broken ring indicates marital problems, but not necessarily divorce. A ring can appear in the coffee grounds of married people, without the marriage or divorce being directly related to the querent. A ring also signifies the pursuit of spiritual enlightenment.

Snail - An interesting formation. A snail generally denotes a passionate, uninhibited sexual nature. A mysterious figure, most of which lies hidden.

Stork - In a woman's cup, a stork indicates virginity, lack of sexual experience - to the point where the querent may even be bothered by it. There is also a connection between the stork and pregnancy or childbirth. A stork with a broken wing in a woman's cup, she does not wish to be pregnant. A stork in a man's cup indicates a fertility problem on his part.

Sword - A significant formation. Always indicates a dispute between individuals who have a lot in common; for instance, a lovers' quarrel. This applies as long as the sword is visible; however, if it is buried in a person's body, this is a serious sign. If the sword is sheathed, it means that the person is not utilizing his talents.

Tiger - A formation that indicates a spirit of adventure, flightiness. In a man's coffee grounds, it also signifies a cruel streak, while for a woman, it points to brazen sexuality.

Tree - A good sign. The person will succeed and flourish, without losing touch with reality. Also a positive symbol for a man or woman suffering from sexual problems: a tree indicates that the solution is close at hand.

Vine - A vine, which usually appears bearing clusters of grapes, is interpreted differently for a man and a woman. When it appears in a man's cup, it is a sign of financial success; in a woman's cup, the interpretation is completely different - sexual problems and inhibitions, lack of sexual satisfaction.

Witch - A common formation. Always signifies another woman who has a significant influence on the querent, whether male or female. It is important to understand that a witch is not necessarily an evil woman. In the cup of a married woman, for example, a witch can symbolize her husband's lover! In a man's cup, this figure often represents his mother-in-law. The formation is interpreted with the help of adjacent shapes.

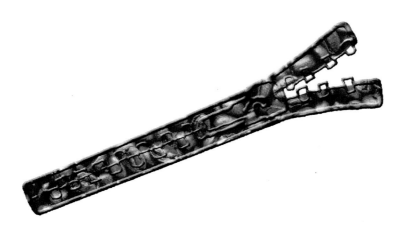

Zipper - A difficult formation. A zipper indicates impotence (even when it appears in a woman's grounds, in which case it refers to the man in her life). The problem is that this is a formation without an answer - we cannot find a reason or a solution in the coffee grounds.

Coffee

A cultural history from around the world

Ed S. Milton

9654941589

Tea

A cultural history from around the world

Ed S. Milton

9654941597

Olive Oil

A cultural history from around the world

Ed S. Milton

9654941600

Wine

A cultural history from around the world

Ed S. Milton

9654941619

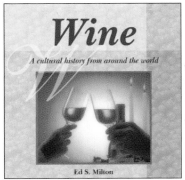